THE TRADITIONAL FEEL OF THE BALLROOM

THE TRADITIONAL FEEL
OF THE BALLROOM

poems by Hannah Gamble

Copyright © July 1, 2021 Hannah Gamble

No part of this book may be used or performed without written consent of the author, if living, except for critical articles or reviews.

Gamble, Hannah
1st edition

ISBN: 978-1-949487-08-4
Library of Congress Control Number: 2021930805

Interior design by Matt Mauch
Cover art by Mariangela LeThanh
Cover design by David Barthwell
Editing by Matt Mauch and Sara Lefsyk

Trio House Press, Inc.
Ponte Vedra Beach, FL

To contact the author, send an email to tayveneese@gmail.com.

*This book is for girls,
and for all the people who are good to them.*

Table of Contents

I
Hanging Out with Girls / 12
I Will Explain Infidelity / 13
Always Given / 14
Cabana / 16
Disrespectful Poem / 18
Penis is a Transitive Verb / 19
The Queen / 21
Edifying Just to See / 22
A Tiny Spot / 24
Indications That Her Honesty / 26
Poetry Must Be Allowed to Heckle / 27
The Sun and Open Air / 28

II
Somewhere Golden / 32
Growing a Bear / 34
Experience as a Tightness / 36
Different Dirt / 38
Holy People / 40
Despite Its Promising Title
The ABCs of Death Proved to Be a Subpar Film / 42
Empty Movie Theater / 44
Weather Today / 46
Cliffs in Arizona / 48
You as Wonderful / 49
I Had the Jokes / 50

III
I Think of My Bicycle as a Kind of Horse / 54
I Wanted to Make Myself like the Ravine / 55
Thing, Pictured / 57
All That is Limitless / 58
It Would Continue / 60
I've Sent My Bigness Clamoring / 62
Most People Would Rather Not / 64

Acknowledgements / 67
About the Author / 69

*. . . how nasty it is to be embodied,
and how better it is
to be nasty than dead.*

– Brandon Brown

*I like playing characters
who have no idea how bad they have it.*

– Cheri Oteri

I

HANGING OUT WITH GIRLS

Hanging out with girls makes me lonely.
There's so much of no one is fat
and he was a dick for saying that
and she was a bitch for not listening
to you better.

Looking at pictures makes me lonely, too:
The time we were g-chatting but I was also crying,
looking at pictures of Eric dancing
with his friend's mom at a wedding.

Someone asked me at a poetry reading
how I got so comfortable talking between poems
and I said that once I went to see some musicians perform
for a birthday, and even when they were playing beautiful Chopin,
they offered something extra, like a little physical
comedy routine built around the playing of the piece.

Since then I've wanted to give people
who come to see poetry a little something extra,
and me, blabbering, is all I've ever had
to give or to keep or to be with on my own.

There's really very little art in that.
You'll never hear me say it's noble.

Or if it is noble, it's only because it isn't fun
to show everyone how little you have
and how little you are.
But no one has much,

and no one is much,
and everyone should know that we share that.

I WILL EXPLAIN INFIDELITY

When you are living in a different part of the country than is your lover,
the one who is right there, and wants you,
is the best one.

Whenever people are surprised that so-and-so has cheated
on a very good-looking person

with a much less good-looking person
I think, *You don't know how cheating works.*

When I wanted a vacation, the whole point was to go
somewhere different, not better.

And when I wanted to hurt one of the small animals
on my father's property I didn't look for the cutest animal.
In fact, when I found an animal that no one else
was paying attention to, I thought my prospective actions less heinous.

I was only broadening a crack
in an already cracked thing,
like choosing the flattened candy bar to steal.

ALWAYS GIVEN

I do not possess that which I produce.

My father reads the *Tao Te Jing*.
My mother makes vases
in the shapes of human heads.

Where does it come from, what comes from me? Elsewhere
my 4 year old dog has just been born.

In the top dresser drawer I had a terrible fight
with my mother when I was 16.
We're just worried no one will like you.

Having been reared in deference and obedience,
I was pushed into a doorway by a man from the pub.

I knew I couldn't fight him off, or that even if I could,
there would be 5 others like him waiting.

I chose to welcome him, in my way.

Other women were nearby
so I wasn't afraid.

He kissed my neck and I said "Oh, yeah,
people tend to like that."

He bit my earlobe and I said "Oh, yeah,
goin' for the ear."

I was trying to be above him.
Above the doorway, above the street.

Above the other women who wouldn't have
"handled it as well."

The women nearby were grinning—in on the joke I was
trying to make of the man.

All of us were mistaken.

Years later I told a friend the funny story of how,
on a french dance floor, a big man in a rain poncho
kept fwapping my hips and ass
with his enormous and erect (though clothed) penis,
and my friend's face widened like an aperture
then fell like an old leaf.

Only upon seeing my friend's face did I see that
I had been mistaken about what was the joke,
and who was the joke.

I tried to, and succeeded in, never making that mistake again
but due to the ever-unfolding nature of the universes
created daily by the curious person,
the opportunities for new mistakes are always given.

CABANA

A cabana is both an "indigenous hut"
and a "recreational structure"
and, in the context of its latter definition,
much like a vagina.

Instead of "pussy,"
now please say "cabana."

You can't keep the weather
out of either. You can't
keep people out of either,
and you can't keep people in.

Mothers want babies out,
once carrying them has become
uncomfortable, but they also
(the mothers) are crying

because they don't want to lose
what seems to belong
inside them;

imagine if your heart
just left your body.
You might feel embarrassed
that your heart had pushed a hole

through your shirt and now everyone
can see your tits a little, but also,
how's that heart going to make it

out there in the horrible world
without you? So many animals
would love to eat it
and so many careless motorists—
texting, reaching for something
deep in the console.
Maybe you feel zero attachment

to the heart but you still feel guilt
when a thing previously in your charge

leaves you and barrels
toward harm.

A vagina is safe,
which is why the most troubled people
must get inside
at any cost.

Outright crimes aside,
almost every woman
has felt rushed.

A man clamoring toward
what he perceives as safety
like a child who becomes
violent when he just
needs sleep or juice.

The men who come so fast
once they enter a vagina—
it's not overstimulation,

it's relief: *Thank god
I can give up
and let a little of my life leak.*

But then what's the woman saying
when she comes?

*He tried to kill me
but then I came back!
(As I will every time
someone tries to kill me,*

*which, I imagine,
will be on the regular.)*

DISRESPECTFUL POEM

I brought my students a poem about rape
and they said they were surprised
I'd disrespected them in that way,
making them read
the work "Fuck" so many times.

I thought I was respecting them
by letting them read a poem
that said *I won't let you fuck me again*,
because I assumed
that some of them had been fucked by people
they never wanted to be fucked by,
not just again, but ever.

I thought I was telling them
they could say *No*
and say so loudly
in the language that
fuckers understand.

PENIS IS A TRANSITIVE VERB

And that is why I have to be a man
in all my poems; I am the subject

because I am the one making
all the things happen

and this is why grammar is one of my favorite things.
I know: there's nothing passive

about a hole. There's nothing
passive about the object to which

happens the verb or to which the preposition
carries the gift. The post was standing still

and the hole worked really hard
to sidle up around it. And then to hold it—

that's never easy. Everything is really
more work than you'd expect:

keeping additional dirt out…
well, that's basically it, but there's

a lot of dirt blown towards a hole.
Metaphors aside, sometimes I think

I better fill me up. So I do,
and then there's no room for anyone

to get inside, so then there's more work to be done.
Becoming a hole again is hard, and it's a service

and a vote of confidence in the other. Some soil's always
lost in each transfer—plenty of back-and-forths

each season, but (lucky for me, and you,
and everyone) there's always things

scraping, aging, crushing, and shitting,
so there's always more dirt.

Do you know what I was like before I met you?
Ignorant. Solitary. Serene. Sort of godlike, in those respects.

THE QUEEN

The queen came to visit me
about my impending
loss of virginity.
The messier the better,
she said.
I know, I said.

But I was thinking that an animal
would be best for the first time—
for practice.

Oh, no, said the queen.
*We reserve animals
for the people who have done it
hundreds of times with humans.*

*Have you done it
with an animal*, I said.
Oh, yes, said the queen.

*Well I was thinking that I should do it
with an animal*, I said.
Just the first time, for practice.

The queen withdrew and escorts
arrived shortly.
They took me to the field
where I was meant
to mate with a tree.
They said I had a poet's
contrary disposition.

EDIFYING JUST TO SEE

When his dick finally
felt right again
and he could pee
without it burning,
he went right back out
into the special places
where the women lived
and were waiting.

Some pulled their dresses
down, like they were ready
to have his dick
go between their tits
like right
now, and some of them
seemed to want a beer first.

The magic of women
just trying to get
something right.

They've usually been taught
that getting a man to come
is the easiest thing—
working a crude tool.

A good thing to do, therefore,
when everything else
that day has proved too challenging.

The man takes one woman
to a private hotel bathroom.
The hotel is the nicest hotel
in all of Houston.

To get to bathroom, they must walk through
what was once a ballroom, all its gold and domes
retained. The woman thinks it's edifying

just to see this kind of place.
The music playing
in the private bathroom
while the man hands her a stack
of paper towels
to wipe off her chest
is more electronic and sexual
than she might have expected
based on the traditional feel
of the ballroom.
The man feels it's best
not to hold the woman's hand
as they leave the hotel, because that
could indicate a tenderness he thinks
it best not to offer. At a bakery
nearby they stop so she can eat
a macaroon, and they get into
a friendly argument about art
that leaves them both
feeling happy.

A TINY SPOT

A tiny spot of blood on my shirt
is not the subject of this poem.
I felt sick
knowing I'd said
what I didn't mean,
and then dreamt about having said
exactly what I meant, and oh, look,
everything worked out fine.

You are wrong if you think
a girl making up her own language
after something that she never wants to talk about
happens to her is the subject of this poem.

I receive emails all the time,
and physical mail too, so don't
tell me that my life isn't full of feeling
cared for and feeling safe,
or, alternatively, knowing that
if in this moment, a gray horse came charging
down Chicago's streets I could stop
that horse in her tracks and ask
for a ride. And be given it.

And not even have to wear a coat
because joy conducts heat
like the perfect thing someone says
when you're upset, though in other
situations it would sound like an insult
but in that moment it's kind
because truth is a service
and a vote of confidence
that you can take it.

You don't even have to clean yourself up very much
for someone who knows you.

Horse, when I saw you charging past
the ice cream vendor, streaming sweat,

eyes mostly white with panic and strength,
anger and exhaustion,
my mind recognized you
and called out to you with my name.

INDICATIONS THAT HER HONESTY

There were indications that her honesty was enough
and was beautiful, fluffed out
like a marigold feeding off

cast-off garbage of the neighbors, corpses of the songbirds
giving up in November. Gorgeous!
But then there were choices, and I don't believe

I ever meant to disclose that my mother's visit
meant so much and so little
to trouble. Everyone begins baking together

means all is forgiven—Oh!

Or the way a wife rolls over so her husband
comes at her again, forgiveness and trouble
and berries being not in season

but showing up anyway in a way that anyone
desperate for signs of harshness dissipating
can look heavenward

where clouds are also missing
and be thankful. We find so little at the hearth
or at bath time, besides the steam that calms

when eucalyptus is introduced for the beauty
of the mind, saying beauty is calm
but the other is sublime

in the way that a horrible woman
with a fine face and animal skins
with the heads still attached and handsome consorts

entering from the front
and behind is beautiful
but the terror trumps this,
to be thankful for.

POETRY MUST BE ALLOWED TO HECKLE

The woman who thinks her clit and her womb
are the most interesting things in the room,

as if they were important on their own (rather than because they are
    attached to her
and in many instances dictate how she relates to others,

when they're down there, with her things,
trying to please her, realizing

that pleasing her will please them, which could be ego
in need of a stroking, or love, some time ago

extant, and maybe now reappearing—tentatively!—over some hill,
looking around to see whether you'll be the first to say hello, or if it will).

Poetry must be allowed to heckle any woman who writes about her thighs
as if they are the pillars to the temple where the covenant lies.

I hear this poem several times a year,
its tone vacillating between reverent and sultry,

but I know I'm in possession of nothing so dear:
once I shaved my crotch and it looked like poultry.

THE SUN AND OPEN AIR

A man is trying to get a woman
to have lunch with him so that he might
eventually secure a source of company
and sex. The woman is hesitant,
so the man tries to excite her
by showing her that he is not
inclined towards jealousy,
nor is he afraid to speak about intimate
events with a near stranger:
The man asks the woman for the details
of her most recent sexual experience, after which
the woman decides not to have lunch with the man.

Classic!! the man is later heard saying
to a group of other men, enacting frustration
with all women who won't even let one get so far as
You can be so much better than she was. Because
did you know that women trying to be better
than other women is the leading cause
of marriage? We already know that men
trying to be better than other men is the cause
of war and that men trying to be better than
women say men are the other leading cause
of marriage. Children come when the couple wants
to be better people than the people they think
they'll be if their lives (and, for example,
expensive sound systems) never get busted open
by a child they immediately love more than anything.

The woman who declined the man's lunch offer
was biologically programed to keep things out.
The man who, rejected, starts calling the woman
"crotch bunch" behind her back thanks
to an unflattering pair of shorts worn at the company cookout,
was biologically programmed to put things in.
I know I was talking about wars earlier—wars
as a male endeavor. But I don't know what to call the thing
where everyone, in accordance with the specifics

of his or her creation, does his or her job exactly right
and everyone suffers, and no one goes out to lunch
and people are mean and ashamed. And women wear skirts
but still try to keep things out and men wear pants
though their dicks are always trying to get out
and see the sun. And nothing, *nothing*
is wrong with that. All living things want the sun
and open air, and if it weren't for dicks,
all vaginas would be naked at the seaside—*always*.

II

SOMEWHERE GOLDEN

One woman said
Clean yourself up
with a cocktail napkin, so here I am
in the bathroom.
Sounds of the party.
Sounds of one man
pretending he gets the joke.
Oh, he gets the joke.
He just didn't think
it was very funny.
I can understand that man.
The bones of Tom's hand
made a fist
and told my nose
a joke, which is to say he
hit me. The resulting laughter
was quiet, but
well-sustained. People decorate
their bathrooms
like I would rather be at the beach
than in this bathroom.
I'd rather be watching swans
mate for life. Well,
not actually mating.
Okay, actually mating;
you can hardly tell
what's going on. Unlike
pornography, or unlike
a wedding ceremony. Or, no.
The wedding ceremony is more
like swans. I thought
I was just watching two people
hold hands
in front of a candle.
The people deciding
to wear flowers in the winter,
disrespectful of what the world
(consistent, opinionated) said we could wear

or eat, like the asparagus hoers d'oeuvres
insisted it was a good time
to feel like it was summer.
At the wedding I was quiet.
At the party I was quiet
until Tom found me
offensive. The homeowners
long ago had decided
I'd rather be somewhere golden
than in this bathroom.
Outside the sounds
of people making promises,
or rather, hushing a room
to condone the most public
of promises made
under an archway.
When I'm cleaned up
I'll find, if he was invited,
the man who played the organ,
or the priest who wears soft shoes
so he doesn't disturb the holy
spirits resting in the rafters
when he walks through
the resting cathedral,
stooping at times
to pick up flowers.

GROWING A BEAR

Growing a bear—a midnight occupation,
the need for which you perhaps first realized
when you saw the wrong kind of shadow

under your chin—a convex when you expected
concave, so now it's clear
you're growing older. Your wife was in the shower

and you wanted to step inside
and soap her up like you did in college when she said

"I'll shower with you, but I'm leaving
my underwear on," and you enjoyed her
in every way you could enjoy a person with soap.

You didn't join your wife in the shower.
She's gotten funny about letting you see her
shave her legs or wash herself anywhere.

You think she read it somewhere—
that letting your husband see you pluck anything,
trim anything, apply medicine to anything,
will make him feel like he's furniture.

It's exactly on cold nights like these that the basement
is not as forbidding as it should be, despite the fact
that you have to put gloves on
in what is part of your own home.

Downstairs, a large bathtub, kept, for some reason,
after remodeling. It is there that your bear will be grown,
by you, though you have no idea how. Probably wishing

is most of it; fertilizer, chunks of raw stew meat,
handfuls of blackberries, two metal rakes, and a thick rug
make up the rest. Then water.

You get an email from a friend late at night

saying he can't sleep. You write back
"I hope you feel sleepy soon" and think how childish
the word "sleepy" is. And you're a man,
older than most of the people you see on television.

You haven't even considered how your wife will feel
when you have finished growing your bear. You could
write a letter to her tonight, explaining how your life
was so lacking in bear.

"Janet, it's nothing you've done——
clearly you have no possible way of supplying me with a bear
or any of the activities I might be able to enjoy
after acquiring the bear."

It might just be best
to keep the two worlds separate.
Janet clearly prefers things to be comfortable
and unchallenging. Janet soaps herself up. Janet puts herself
to bed, and you just happen to be next to her.

You go on your weekly bike ride with Mark and tell him
that you've been growing a bear. An eighteen-wheeler
flies by and he doesn't seem to hear you—
plus he's focused on the hill.

You think about how not all friends know
what each other sounds like when struggling and
breathing heavy. Past the age of college athletics,
most friends don't even know what each others' bodies
look like, flushed, tired, showering, cold.

EXPERIENCE AS A TIGHTNESS

It's not exactly that someone has died
or even that, surrounded by tiny potted
plants sent to the farmhouse
in prospective sympathy, they will die.
It's instead that the collar, buttoned as a choice
to look clean and like the day is no threat,
makes this weight exactly
where I don't want it,
as I try to think that breathing
is no difficult thing, that life is absolutely
a door that someone opened to give me
a lovely time, a period of eighty years
or so wherein I will be allowed
to experience love, and be given
so much love that I sometimes will have
to step back, don a grandpa sweater-vest kind of
head-shaking smile, and say *Thank you,
I've got to sit down*, and of course
everyone would understand
that they'd done well. They'd done such
a good job of loving me that my heart
had hardly enough elastic, was hardly prepared.
It's just that all my clothes seem to keep
me from breathing, even my shoes.
It's good to look around
and see the ways other people manage to forget
about what they surely must
experience as a tightness.
This one searches for the most beautiful
tie clips online—another might approach
the receptionist's desk to talk about how
he's a pretty good singer; people always
tell him so. What I'd like to know is why
parties, holidays, and parades always leave me
thinking that it's kind of intimate, dealing with
other people's garbage. The same person
who would jerk back if she thought
I was about to touch her would still

let me carry her cup to the kitchen
when her mouth's been all over it.

DIFFERENT DIRT

A little bit of blood on the hand,

A little bit of pee in the snow.

A little bit of soup on your sweater—you were trying to drink
the soup from a mug in the car.

A little bit of relief when your spouse's return home
is delayed by a snowstorm.

A little bit of pride—you were just 18—when a coworker
told you you were "funny like a guy is funny."

A little bit of exhaustion when someone looking at you naked
tells you you're beautiful.

A little bit of anger, always.

Let's retire to tiny cottages in the wilderness
and be done with it (each other).

Currently, interpersonal disputes
are taxes on the body,

out of which the spirit will climb,
trying to escape.

Half in, half out,
the spirit flaps above the body's headlike a windsock.

SOME DISPUTES BETWEEN LOVERS CANNOT BE RESOLVED,
so flee!

SOME DISPUTES BETWEEN LOVERS over whose floor lamp is uglier
CANNOT BE RESOLVED because the two separate realities

of both strong-headed,
well-educated lovers are so firmly contrary:

different trees growing out of different dirt
in different countries.

HOLY PEOPLE

After a very bad thing happens
it may feel like you will never
call your mother back.

The bathroom was quiet and well-lit,
and you hid there.

It's not that anyone was being unkind,
it's just that it had been hours of talking
without intensity or connection.

Newspaper articles
are beginning to discuss
what it means to hide in bathrooms.

Hiding because someone insulted you in a faculty meeting
is different than hiding because there's been too much talk
and too little of everything else.

When you wake up,
that's when the mosquito begins.

You might be a holy person.

Holy people never feel at home,
so they make trouble for everyone
while looking exhausted.

In any case,
I hope you'll come outside again soon.

Mostly you have to stop worshipping the idea
of you being horrible.

I like you better than almost anyone,
and the fact that you don't agree
that you're worth something
hurts my feelings.

I've never had to tell you
why we write—you always seemed to know it.
But I guess there are other things
you think you know,
and it's not really up to me to change your mind.
I still tried, though, didn't I?
A prehistoric woman with swinging breasts,
banging and banging on a coconut.

DESPITE ITS PROMISING TITLE,
THE ABCs OF DEATH PROVED TO BE A SUBPAR FILM

And so began my 30th year,
signaled by tiny explosions
out the rear of my cap gun; me,
standing in Tim's front yard,
shooting up into the dim screen
of the stars washed out
by city lights.

There are times when you want a new thing
so badly you might find yourself
screaming into your friend's couch cushion
while he's in the bathroom.

Without novelty or challenge
an organism more often than not
assumes its death shroud.

When a banana is more brown
than yellow, the *air* is all
that's bruising it.

When an organism perceives its inutility
it removes itself from the equation
for the greater good, just like when
I get really quiet at parties.

Why do *you* think so many
writers write about parties?
Probably because it's so hard for anything
to grow there. Parties are like
allegorical representations of everything
humans are capable of
but grown in the most shallow petri dishes.

Have you ever noticed how a thing
can mean two things?
I realized that on my 30th birthday,

when my friend offered me a salad upon which
he'd lovingly piled papaya
and also began to hate me a little bit
because I hadn't come inside sooner
to help him set the table.

EMPTY MOVIE THEATER

There are days when everything you think you are
decides to cool it.

You tell your friend to take you
to the suburbs so you can experience his dog and his house

and his parents who come home in time
to meet you and order a pizza.

Other days, you just want a vibrating cock ring
and a friend who'll forgive

every sappy, desperate thing you say
while you're inside her.

You want to go to your college friend's wedding,
but there will be too many people there

who don't want to see you; no one will be able
to act normally—they are artistic and extremely

intelligent, living their lives with enough
self-awareness to electrocute a pig

and enough self-loathing to desiccate
all the fat and muscle of a fringe-wearing professional wrestler.

If you think there's no one more like a blister,
I ask you to consider the mental/emotional counterpart

to the greased-up wrestler's body;
and now we're back, in Houston, TX,

with the writers—everyone drunk, everyone
being all the funny smart allows.

You remember meeting them and thinking
you'd found what your stepmother would call "your tribe."

You'd learned about tribes in an anthropology class:
Sometimes it's the person who never shares

the meat he caught who's called a witch
and sent away to starve, and sometimes

it's the king who wasn't able to keep his promises.
Some tribes hate braggarts the most,

and some tribes hate the man who only knows one joke
or always tells the same story of the same girl

who loved him immediately, gave him happiness,
and never became any less wonderful.

You have to wonder how any tribe survives,
sending away so many of its own.

The answer: most tribes have a holy man who keeps a basket,
and inside that basket is every sound

the exiled make when stepping on a stone in the night
or being frightened by a tree branch.

The tribespeople are kept company by these noises and,
after listening, often feel as if they've eaten a large meal.

WEATHER TODAY

For I am not without
a perceivable amount
of guilt and grief
with which I address
from my far away place
you, my friend, as set
to the sound of a television
delivering some news
across a winter sea.
Set to the tune
of repetitive piano music
you are beautiful,
and I might have told you so
a year ago
as the glory of the health food store
shone all around us
and the large healthy women
smelled warm.
There alone now,
anytime without you
I defy your request
to never find myself
eating alone.
Now anyone passing
sees me bent
under the nothing
of some day,
whereas if you were here,
they would see me
leaning in to better hear you.
Today's letter
must stick to essentials:
Today's weather
is nets of water draped over shrubbery.
My human body
feels caught up in wind.
I flail about,

praising it. Rather servile.
You might say begging.

CLIFFS IN ARIZONA

– After a line by James Wright

When I went out to kill myself it really
wasn't because of anything you'd done.

I regret, mostly, not leaving when I wanted to—
your dick would have rowed you through

the world like a paddle—
there was no chance of me hurting you.

The thing about women, though,
is that we're horses who twist up

and break our ankles
trying not to step on the rider

who's fallen to the ground.
Then we'll put the gun

in your hand when we know we're no longer
any good on the track.

Being a woman the way that I was a woman
meant knowing your clothes were too big for me,

but still wanting to cut all the fat
off my stomach with scissors.

Ending it in a café, you meant to imply
you cared about me some,

so you said something about my body
and the good it did you.

That night I thought about how, if I chewed off my hand,
I could have placed it on my ass as I slept.

YOU AS WONDERFUL

The most amazing thing is that I'm still able to remember you
as wonderful. Even when not in your bed, I was always in your bed:

at a party, or a picnic table with friends, I was remembering
your shaded room where I was untying your shoes,

and pulling my hair back so you could see my face.
This did realer things to me than I was used to.

Back when you were wonderful, I held your hand
at the hospital, when they put a needle

the size of a milkshake straw in your spine.
Our friend had asked if he should come too, and you said *No,*

only Hannah. The bed rocked forward and back
when they screwed the needle in.

I passed out and then stood back up and found your hand
and passed out again.

I woke up and told you I was using sign language
for "I can't feel my hands." The doctors laughed softly

and said I shouldn't have come.
The morphine held you then and I called our friend.

He's doing fine, and I'm crying a little bit. I laughed a little
on the phone. You said *Hey, Hannah Gamble—*
I'll hold your hand.

I HAD THE JOKES

So often it's the man
I thought was a sure bet
who says the meanest things
once we've ended.

*MY MOM WAS ALWAYS ASKING ME
WHY I WAS WITH YOU.*

*YOU ONLY AGREED
TO BE MY GIRLFRIEND
SO I WOULD HELP YOU MOVE.*

*YOU AREN'T EVEN GOOD AT
SHOWING LOVE TO YOUR DOG.*

Funny, my mom
always likes these men the best.

She thinks, rightly,
that they're sensitive and sweet.

She likes that they're quiet,
and not too noticeably funny.

She's not intimidated
or confused by them.

She cheerfully suggests marriage
five months in.

But despite all this
she never questions
my reasons for ending things.

She just hadn't seen
what was happening,
and couldn't know.

She liked how the men didn't try to scold me
or control me.

I looked vibrant, happy, in charge,
she'd say.

And I'd say yes, I was in charge,
because they were incapable.

I had the car, I had the brains.
I had the butt, I had the book.
I had the voice, I had the plan.
I had a bad feeling about it. I had the jokes.

III

I THINK OF MY BICYCLE AS A KIND OF HORSE

I think of my bicycle as a kind of horse
that lets me push the neighborhood wind
away with my face—a kind of horse
accessible to children and criminal men
no longer allowed to drive cars.

Here is the sidewalk where I ran through wet cement
and fell only partially down. This is my town,
though bad things have happened to me here.

No matter who injures me,
I think that people are entitled to their feelings.

If a man doesn't have looks, health, or money,
when he gets mad, you want to let him have it.

A bicycle is a kind of horse upon which
I can feel incredibly alone—
enough to address a greater thing
as the neighborhood at dusk
gives me a feeling.

The only prayer
I ever pray goes like this: *Hey! Thing!*
Your presence is fact,
and your name and your face
are things you have never wanted me to see
or reach towards.

I WANTED TO MAKE MYSELF LIKE THE RAVINE

I wanted to make myself like the ravine
so that all good things
would flow into me.

Because the ravine is lowly,
it receives an abundance.

This sounds wonderful
to everyone who suffers
from lacking,
but consider, too, that a ravine
keeps nothing out:

In flows a peach
with only one bite taken out of it,
but in flows too
the body of a stiff mouse
half cooked by the heat of the stove
it was toughening under.

I have an easygoing way about me.
I've been an inviting host—
meaning to, not meaning to.
Oops—he's approaching with his tongue
already out
and moving.

Analyze the risks
of becoming a ravine.

Compare those with the risks
of becoming a well
with a well-bolted lid.

Which I'd prefer
depends largely on which kinds
of animals were inside
when the lid went on

and how likely they'd be
to enjoy the water,
vs. drown, or freeze, or starve.

The lesson: close yourself off
at exactly the right time.

On the day that you wake up
under some yellow curtains
with a smile on your face,

lock the door.
Live out your days
untroubled like that.

THING, PICTURED

Ash scatters across the table, past an uncomplicated display
of plant arrangements.
Small things, collected, can be more
than enough.

When my brother was not much younger,
he made a picture of my sister's face
using only ink
and, on not even very special paper, his fingerprints.

ALL THAT IS LIMITLESS

I usually wake up with acquisition
in mind.

I make myself the tallest pine;
I have more birds on me
than anybody!

The sun hits my head
first—it's cooled a bit
by the time it gets to your head.

I thought I'd get the most

if all the good saw me first
and affably went there.

It was sound,
my lightning rod approach.

One oversight
was that when the bad was coming
it also saw me first,

and would match its force
to my height in a way
that, I'm sure, if I had a stutter
or a limp
would be lessened.

In any case,
it's time to get lowly.

Put on a formless gown
and call it a shroud
for your vanity, a gold braid
on your forehead

or a word you have
to explain
to everyone at the table.

Even if it wasn't vanity, but hunger.
Even if it was mostly enthusiasm
and affectionate regard. An invitation
to join (less like "participate"
and more like "become an actual part of,"
cutting a part off so it fits
more snugly with the other part).

Now you have a bed.
Now you have a table.

If the wood is still living
we'll make not furniture
but a living structure:
We can do what we call grafting.
This too requires a bit of cutting.

A dormant bud
can be cut and grafted,
as can a young shoot,
but in all cases
the point of vascular connection can end up weak
due to the varying strengths
of the two formerly distinct tissues.

Once I blew my nose in a cafe
despite the number of approximate men
in beautiful sweaters and I knew
I'd become another thing.

*Now when a block is sawed up
it is made into implements.*

*The finest sculptor carves
the least. In this way,
the block rests
within all that is limitless.*

IT WOULD CONTINUE

Rough skin on my big toe
when I move it to make sure
some part of me
is touching you while we sleep.

Once we had a fight
that you still say was just
a tough conversation.

To me, it sounded cold
and flat when you said
"Go on, hit the lights,"
and so whenever you moved your hand
or foot towards me,
I moved closer to the wall,
thinking you were asking me
for space.

You didn't accept that.
You explained in the morning.

I felt relieved,
and came to understand you
as someone who will stay close
even when angry.

I knew years ago,
in a different city altogether,
that I was done with feelings,
or that they weren't enough.

A different man saying
"I feel so awful

I couldn't keep my promise
to you," and me saying
"I don't want to know
about your feelings,

I want you to change
your behavior."

That moment led that man
to call me the slow-moving iceberg
that would crush
the lowly scrub pine.

You asked me what he meant.

I explained that in that moment
he'd seen a cold,
glowing orb in my center.
It didn't not love him,
it just had no idea
that he existed.

It would continue.
It was pure will.

It would continue,
and would crush
anything that didn't move
or join it.

I've felt you join me.
I've felt me joining you.

Sometimes we don't talk much,
or look at each other;

You retrieve my bike helmet.
I unlock your bike from the post.

I'VE SENT MY BIGNESS CLAMORING

I have been less than I could be.
I let a symbol be a symbol when a symbol's

not enough. Good is the thing I stopped
trying to be but you are where I want
to put every good thing about me.

Even today, the wind makes it hard
for us to talk to one another.
If the world is ending

it's only because we let the trees
be only symbols or because we presided over.
My mother begins cheering

for the life I finally admit to wanting:
a life where someone is allowed to love me
because I've moved something in me aside

to make room for that love. She's right to cheer,
as anyone who wants to affirm two people

touching in absolute terror of touching is right
to say it is good to leave your country bed for whatever song

injured animals use to grieve and ask politely
where the raspberries are. When the Austrian monk

began sleeping with the French nun he was also right.
My eyes were moving through the air

and I was trying to talk to you in spite of the wind.

Settling for talking to others about you
was a thing I no longer would settle for.

Believing in the coming rain without holding
out my hand is an act of fear

and an act of laziness. Beside the bigness of the trees

I am a smaller kind of big. Exhausted, rough,
ceasing, somehow, to be intelligent,

I must have decided you were worth it.

Look at my face and tell me which parts of it
you'd like to keep with you,
with my blessing and with my forever apologies

for being less than every good I want for you.
I've sent my bigness clamoring up this tree
to burst into seed and be much better

in one hundred years.
Something the town will commemorate.

MOST PEOPLE WOULD RATHER NOT

Most people would rather not,
but I indulge, every few weeks,
the thought of it.

Sometimes the oily smell of an evening flower appears
and hangs in the air,
a slightly browner spot.

I think most people had it wrong when they said
forget about it and find a fresh patch
of grass to lie down in.

There are prayers, though,
about that kind of peace.

I have to admit,
sometimes I want nothing more than to be lying on the bottom
of an unimpressive river.

I can watch all the leaves and sticks skim over my head,
and no one will bother me
because they're swimming
in the more impressive rivers.

The water's not too cold. It doesn't feel
like being dead.

It also doesn't feel like being old
or fetal.

I came to the humble water to lie down.

I did what I set out to do.

Now I don't have to tell you
anything more about it.

Notes

p. 59: The italicized stanzas are excerpeted from the *Doa De Jing*.

Acknowledgements

First: thanks so much to the editors of Trio House Press (especially Matt Mauch) for loving this book and giving it a home.

I also want to say thank you to all of the poets, photographers, painters, sketchers, musicians, and playwrights who have let my work be part of your creative life by making work inspired by mine.

Thank you, too, to the educators (at high school military academies, fine arts schools, after school programs, community colleges, and universities) who have shared my work with your students.

Now the more personal thank-yous:

Tavius and Ashley: I can never express exactly and weightily enough how much it means to spend time with you. You both are brilliant, talented, funny, so thoughtful, and so kind to me. You inspire, educate, encourage, and loudly cheer for me. I love you.

Russell, Laaura, Kayla, Andrew, and Sean: My Chicago babes—thanks for supporting my creative work, checking in, sharing your homes/food/thoughts/animal companions/drugs with me, celebrating with me, and (occasionally, when necessary) grieving with me. Your friendship means so much and I'm so proud be your friend.

•

The following poems first appeared in these journals:

Barrelhouse Review, "I Had the Jokes"; "Different Dirt"

Pleiades, "Penis is a Transitive Verb"; "Poetry Must Be Allowed to Heckle"

The Southeast Review, "The Sun and Open Air"; "Despite Its Promising Title, *The ABCs of Death* Proved to Be a Subpar Film"

POETRY, "I Wanted to Make Myself like the Ravine"; "Growing a Bear"; "Most People Would Rather Not"

American Poetry Review, "Hanging Out with Girls"; "I Will Explain Infidelity"

Ampersand Review, "Weather Today"; "Holy People"

The Academy of American Poets / *Poem-a-Day*, "All That is Limitless"

The Believer, "Cabana"

Black Warrior Review, "The Queen"; "A Tiny Spot"; "Indications That Her Honesty"

Court Green, "I Think of My Bicycle as a Kind of Horse"; "You as Wonderful"; "Cliffs in Arizona"

Coldfront, "Disrespectful Poem"

Forklift, Ohio, "I've Sent my Bigness Clamoring"

jubilat, "Somewhere Golden"

About the Author

Hannah Gamble is a poet, essayist, screenwriter, and director. Her first book of poems, *Your Invitation to a Modest Breakfast*, won the National Poetry Series in 2011. In 2014, she received the Ruth Lilly/Dorothy Sargent Rosenberg fellowship from the Poetry Foundation. She is the writer, director, and executive producer of the Chicago-based webseries *Choose Me: An Abortion Story*, which was selected for several national and international film festivals, winning the Award of Excellence for a TV Show from the Montreal Independent Film Festival in 2020.

About the Book

The Traditional Feel of the Ballroom
was designed at Trio House Press through the collaboration of:

Matt Mauch, Lead Editor
Sara Lefsyk, Supporting Editor
David Barthwell, Cover Design
Matt Mauch, Interior Design

The text is set in Adobe Caslon Pro.

The publication of this book is made possible, whole or in part, by the generous support of the following individuals or agencies:

Anonymous

About the Press

Trio House Press is an independent literary press publishing three or more collections of poems annually. Our Mission is to promote poetry as a literary art enhancing culture and the human experience. We offer two annual poetry awards: the Trio Award for First or Second Book for emerging poets and the Louise Bogan Award for Artistic Merit and Excellence for a book of poems contributing in an innovative and distinct way to poetry. We also offer an annual open reading period for manuscript publication.

Trio House Press adheres to and supports all ethical standards and guidelines outlined by the CLMP.

Trio House Press, Inc. is dedicated to the promotion of poetry as literary art, which enhances the human experience and its culture. We contribute in an innovative and distinct way to poetry by publishing emerging and established poets, providing educational materials, and fostering the artistic process of writing poetry. For further information, or to consider making a donation to Trio House Press, please visit us online at www.triohousepress.org.

Other Trio House Press books you might enjoy:

Third Winter in Our Second Country by Andres Rojas / 2021

Sweet Beast by Gabriella R. Tallmadge / 2020 Louise Bogan Award Winner selected by Sandy Longhorn

Songbox by Kirk Wilson / 2020 Trio Award Winner selected by Malena Mörling

YOU DO NOT HAVE TO BE GOOD by Madeleine Barnes / 2020

X-Rays and Other Landscapes by Kyle McCord / 2019

Threed, This Road Not Damascus by Tamara J. Madison / 2019

My Afmerica by Artress Bethany White / 2018 Trio Award Winner selected by Sun Yung Shin

Waiting for the Wreck to Burn by Michele Battiste / 2018 Louise Bogan Award Winner selected by Jeff Friedman

Cleave by Pamel Johnson Parker / 2018 Trio Award Winner selected by Jennifer Barber

Two Towns Over by Darren C. Demaree / 2018 Louise Bogan Award Winner selected by Campbell McGrath

Bird~Brain by Matt Mauch / 2017

Dark Tussock Moth by Mary Cisper / 2016 Trio Award Winner selcted by Bhisham Bherwani

The Short Drive Home by Joe Osterhaus / 2016 Louise Bogan Award Winner selected by Chard DeNiord

Break the Habit by Tara Betts / 2016

Bone Music by Stephen Cramer / 2015 Louise Bogan Award Winner selected by Kimiko Hahn

Rigging a Chevy into a Time Machine and Other Ways to Escape a Plague by Carolyn Hembree / 2015 Trio Award Winner selected by Neil Shepard

Magpies in the Valley of Oleanders by Kyle McCord / 2015

Your Immaculate Heart by Annmarie O'Connell / 2015

The Alchemy of My Mortal Form by Sandy Longhorn / 2014 Louise Bogan Award Winner selected by Peter Campion

What the Night Numbered by Bradford Tice / 2014 Trio Award Winner selected by Carol Frost

Flight of August by Lawrence Eby / 2013 Louise Bogan Award Winner selected by Joan Houlihan

The Consolations by John W. Evans / 2013 Trio Award Winner selected by Mihaela Moscaliuc

Fellow Odd Fellow by Stephen Riel / 2013

Clay by David Groff / 2012 Louise Bogan Award Winner selected by Michael Waters

Gold Passage by Iris Jamahl Dunkle / 2012 Trio Award Winner selected by Ross Gay

If You're Lucky Is a Theory of Mine by Matt Mauch / 2012

www.ingramcontent.com/pod-product-compliance
Lightning Source LLC
Chambersburg PA
CBHW030351100526
44592CB00010B/916